MW00886304

This notebook belongs to

Made in the USA
Monee, IL
20 March 2023

30212786R20061